ROBOTS AND ROBOTICS

Scientific and Medical Robots

Tony Hyland

Smart Apple Media

Smart Apple Media
2140 Howard Drive West
North Mankato, Minnesota 56003

First published in 2007 by
MACMILLAN EDUCATION AUSTRALIA PTY LTD
627 Chapel Street, South Yarra, Australia 3141

Visit our Web site at www.macmillan.com.au or go directly to www.macmillanlibrary.com.au

Associated companies and representatives throughout the world.

Copyright © Tony Hyland 2007

Library of Congress Cataloging-in-Publication Data

Hyland, Tony.
    Scientific and medical robots / by Tony Hyland.
    p. cm. — (Robots and robotics)
    Includes index.
    ISBN 978-1-59920-118-4
    1. Robotics in medicine—Juvenile literature. 2. Robotics—Scientific applications—Juvenile
    literature. 3. Research—Juvenile literature. 4. Scientific apparatus and instruments—Juvenile literature. I. Title.

    R859.7.C67H95 2007
    610.28—dc22

                                                                            2007004743

Edited by Margaret Maher
Text and cover design by Ivan Finnegan, iF Design
Page layout by Ivan Finnegan, iF Design
Photo research by Legend Images

Printed in U.S.

Acknowledgements

The author and the publisher are grateful to the following for permission to reproduce copyright material:

Front cover photograph: Prescription-filling robot at work in the National Naval Medical Center, Maryland, by U.S. Navy, Chief Warrant Officer 4 Seth Rossman.

Photos courtesy of:
© age fotostock/Dinodia, p. 15; © age fotostock/Javier Larrea, p. 5; SelecT, automated cell culture system from The Automation Partnership, Cambridge, UK, p. 9; © Ed Kashi/Corbis, p. 18; Robotic home assistant Care-O-bot II © Fraunhofer IPA, p. 16; © 2007 Honda Motor Company, pp. 24, 25; Aaron Edsinger, Humanoid Robotics Group, p. 23; © 2007 Intuitive Surgical, Inc., pp. 19, 21; Star Trek/Movie Store Collection Ltd, p. 29; © Neuronics AG, p. 6; Ossur, p. 14; Photolibrary/Colin Cuthbert/Science Photo Library, p. 20; Photolibrary/Mauro Fermariello/Science Photo Library, p. 8; Photolibrary/Jerry Mason/Science Photo Library, p. 12; Photolibrary/Maximilian Stock Ltd/Science Photo Library, pp. 7, 27; Photolibrary/Sam Ogden/Science Photo Library, p. 22; Photolibrary/Scott Sinklier/AGSTOCKUSA/Science Photo Library, p. 11; Photolibrary/Pasquale Sorrentino/Science Photo Library, p. 26; Photolibrary/TEK Image/Science Photo Library, p. 10; © Toshiyuki Aizawa/Reuters/Picture Media, p. 17; © Kimimasa Mayama/Reuters/Picture Media, p. 28; Robodoc® Surgical Assistance System, p. 13; U.S. Navy, Chief Warrant Officer 4 Seth Rossman, pp. 1, 4.

Background textures courtesy of Photodisc.

Contents

GLOSSARY WORDS

When a word is printed in **bold**, you can look up its meaning in the glossary on page 31.

Robots

There are more and more robots in the world. Once they were just figments of the imagination, metal creatures that clanked through old **science fiction** movies and books. Robots today are real, and you will find them in the most surprising places. Some are tiny, no bigger than a fly. Others are among the largest machines on Earth.

Robots are machines that can move and think for themselves. Most robots work in factories, doing endless, repeated tasks faster than any human. Other robots explore places that humans cannot safely reach. Some robots go to the bottom of the sea. Others go to the rocky surface of Mars.

There are also **surgical robots**, robots that carry out scientific experiments, and robots that **disarm** bombs. Today's toys often include robot technology—you can even **program** your own toy robot.

Where do robots fit into your life?

The AutoScript robot works in a hospital, collecting medicines for patients.

Scientific and medical robots

Robots are the most complicated and advanced machines in the world. They are designed and built by experienced scientists and engineers. Some of the most intelligent robots work in scientific **laboratories**. They perform thousands of tests without ever becoming tired or bored.

Medical robots are beginning to appear in hospitals. Robots can help perform delicate heart **surgery** on patients. Other robots work as assistants for nursing staff. They can also help take care of elderly patients in nursing homes. Robotic technology is changing life for people who have lost arms or legs.

The science of robotics is exciting and important. Scientists and engineers working in robotics are developing machines that will change our way of life. This book looks at how robots are used in science and medicine, and at what may come in the future.

Robotics engineers work on improving robots.

Robots in the laboratory

Research in laboratories is often slow and boring. Scientists sometimes repeat the same procedures over and over. This is an ideal job for robots. They can do the same tasks again and again without making mistakes.

Mechanical arms

The earliest laboratory robots were mechanical arms, which handled **radioactive material**. Laboratories still use systems like this for handling dangerous substances. Today's robotic arms can be programmed to perform very complicated tasks.

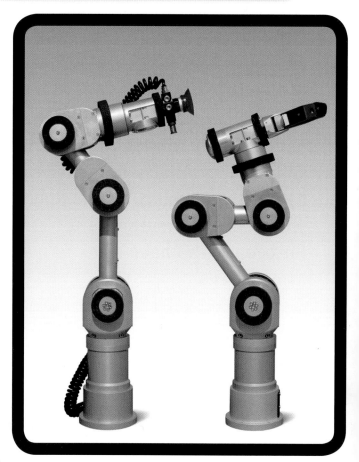

The Katana HD6M robot works in scientific laboratories.

Single-armed lab robot

The Katana HD6M is a robot with one arm and several joints. It can be used in research to handle electronic chips and pour out exact doses of chemicals. It is the only industrial robotic arm that can be used safely around people with no additional protections.

ROBOFACT

LABORATORY ASSISTANTS

Laboratory assistants prepare samples and clean test tubes and other tools. One mistake can ruin an experiment. Laboratory robots can do much of this work over and over without making mistakes.

Clean room robots

Robots can work with materials that would be dangerous to humans. Robots are not affected by viruses, bacteria, radioactive material, or chemicals. They often work in **clean rooms**.

No humans allowed

Human workers stay outside the clean room. They dress from head to toe in protective clothing to avoid **contaminating** the materials. The robot inside the clean room can mix, pour, and sort substances. The materials that the robot produces are guaranteed to be pure. They are not contaminated by bacteria or any other substances.

Silicon chips

The **silicon chips** used in computers are made in clean rooms. Robots manufacture large discs containing thousands of computer chips. The robots then cut the discs into tiny pieces that will each become the central processor in a computer. This is the part which controls all the computer's functions. The tiniest speck of dust on a silicon chip can make it useless.

Robots are often used in clean rooms, as they do not contaminate materials.

Blood testing and growing cells

Scientists often need to test blood samples. They also need to grow animal and plant cells for research. A robot is ideal for these jobs.

Blood testing

Doctors send blood samples to laboratories to be tested for disease. A robot can read the labels on the samples and inject the correct chemicals. It can store the samples and record the results.

Test plates

Many laboratory tests use **test plates** with 96 small test tubes. Several robots work together to handle these tests, including:

- ⚛ liquid-handling robots, which squirt exact amounts of liquid into each tube
- ⚛ plate-mover robots, which move the plates on to the next test
- ⚛ plate-reader robots, which examine the plates and record the results

ROBOFACT

FREEZING WORK

Robots can work in places that would be uncomfortable for humans. Laboratory samples are often frozen. Laboratory robots can load and unload frozen samples without getting cold!

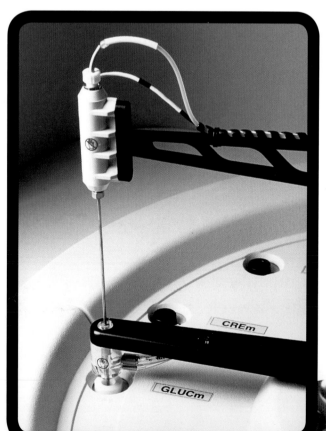

This robotic arm tests blood samples.

Growing cells

In the latest medical research, laboratories grow groups of animal or plant cells. This process is called cell culture. It can be used for creating new drugs, or to cure diseases. The cells must be perfect and uncontaminated, so the work is done by robots in clean rooms.

Cell culture robot

SelecT is a huge, automatic clean room, with several built-in robots for making cell cultures. The robots handle all of the cell cultures inside the machine. Human operators observe and control the process from outside. SelecT is in fact one huge robot, with many working sections.

Future robots

New medicines and genetic materials will be developed in the coming years. Robots such as SelecT will be replaced by factories which use the same processes. Hundreds of robots will work together to produce the materials. Everything that happens inside the factory will be free from human or other contamination.

Robots do all the work inside the SelecT robotic cell-culturing machine.

Robot research

Researchers are always trying to make robots that are better than the ones in use already. They also find new jobs for robots to do.

Improved sensors

The first robots used in scientific research were simple arms. Modern laboratory robots have built-in sensors. They have much better control over the objects they handle.

Improved intelligence

Robots are controlled by computers. As larger, faster computers develop, new robots become much more intelligent. A modern robot can test many different items at the same time and record all the results accurately.

Improved construction

Modern robots move and stop very quickly. This could wear out parts, so robots today are made of new materials that will stay strong for many years.

Laboratory robots can test many samples at the same time.

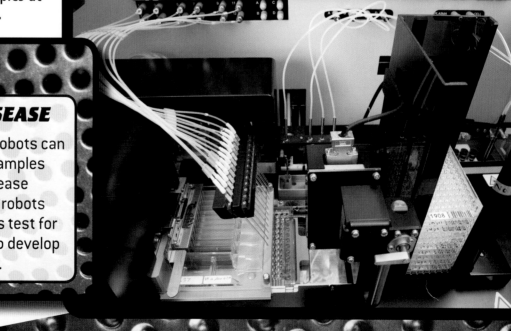

ROBOFACT

STOPPING DISEASE

Modern laboratory robots can test thousands of samples quickly. If a new disease appears, laboratory robots will help researchers test for the disease and help develop new drugs to cure it.

New jobs for robots

Early scientific robots mostly tested blood for diseases. The latest robotic laboratory systems can do new jobs. They can help find new drugs, examine **DNA**, and develop new plants. There are now different testing kits for many types of laboratories. The robots look similar, but the equipment they use is quite different.

Animal research laboratories

Researchers have adapted robotic equipment to animal research. Animal researchers search for drugs that can cure animal diseases. They also look at animal DNA, to find ways to develop larger and healthier farm animals.

Robotic laboratories in space

Robots allow researchers to test materials on other planets. The robots that go to Mars carry advanced testing instruments. They take samples of the soil and then test them. This helps researchers see exactly what substances the planet is made of.

Scientists can use robotic equipment to examine DNA.

Robotic surgery

Surgeons perform operations on humans. In the last few years, surgeons have begun using robots for difficult tasks.

First attempts

The first robotic surgery was done in 1985 with the PUMA 560. It placed a needle inside a patient's brain. This was a delicate task which needed to be done very carefully.

In 1992, surgeons began using Robodoc in hip replacement surgery. Robodoc drills out the damaged bone in the patient's leg. The surgeon replaces the bone with a new section made of metal.

Modern robotic surgery

Today, robots are used in many operations. The robot makes very small **incisions**, while the surgeon controls it from a video screen. Because the cuts are small, patients heal much faster.

The PUMA 560 was originally used in factories, but it later became the first surgical robot.

ROBOFACT

REMOTE SURGERY

Surgeons can now perform robotic surgery from thousands of miles away. The surgeon controls the robot through a computer link. In 2001, a surgeon in the United States operated on a patient in France!

Up Close

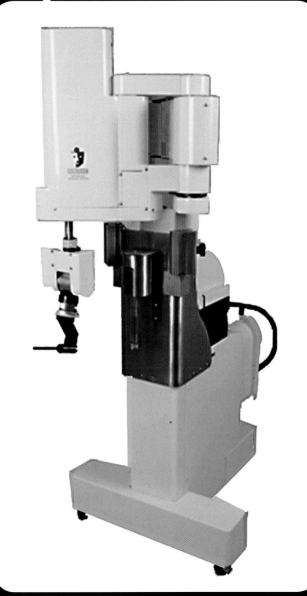

ROBOT
Robodoc

JOB
Surgical robot

MAKER
Integrated Surgical Systems, U.S.

SKILLS
Bone drilling for hip or knee replacement

FIRST USED
1992

Robodoc is a surgical robot. It is a large machine, mounted on wheels. It can be wheeled into an operating room whenever it is needed.

Robodoc's job is only a part of the surgical procedure. First the surgeon makes the necessary incisions to remove the damaged bone. Then Robodoc drills a hole into the remaining bone. It has **pressure sensors** that send messages to the onboard computer. This tells it exactly how far to drill.

Finally, the surgeon places a new hip or knee joint into the drilled out section. Then the surgeon completes the operation by closing up the wound. This operation is much neater than earlier hip or knee operations. Patients are able to leave the hospital earlier, with a new hip or knee.

Artificial limbs

In the past, anyone who lost an arm or leg had it replaced with a clumsy **artificial limb**. Today, scientists can make robotic artificial limbs.

Once, the only artificial limbs were wooden legs and metal hooks. Most artificial limbs today look quite real, but wearers still cannot control them the way they control their other limbs.

Robotic artificial limbs

Robotic artificial limbs behave more like real limbs. The Rheo Knee is made by a company called Ossur. It is an artificial knee that connects to an artificial leg. Its built-in computer learns the person's walking style, and adapts to walking across different types of ground. It automatically adjusts when the person is walking up or down stairs.

ROBOFACT

CONNECTING NERVES TO A ROBOT

Scientists in the U.S. have connected a robotic arm to a monkey's brain. The monkey can control the arm simply by thought. Researchers are now creating these limbs for humans, too.

Although this athlete has lost a leg, he can run easily with his robotic artificial leg.

Next step

The next step is to make artificial limbs that are controlled by the wearer's nerves. Most people move without needing to think about it. Researchers are working on robotic artificial limbs that will work like this, too. Some people have already been fitted with the first robotic artificial limbs.

Artificial hands

In science fiction movies, we see robotic limbs that look and work just like real limbs. Technology today is not that far advanced, but it is getting closer. There are already artificial hands with fingers that move. These hands contain tiny, battery-powered motors, controlled by movements in the wearer's arm muscles.

Sense of touch

Human skin contains millions of tiny nerves that can feel pressure, heat, and texture. These give us our sense of touch. Robotics researchers are developing new fabrics that have this sense. In the next few years we may see artificial limbs that will give their wearers a sense of touch.

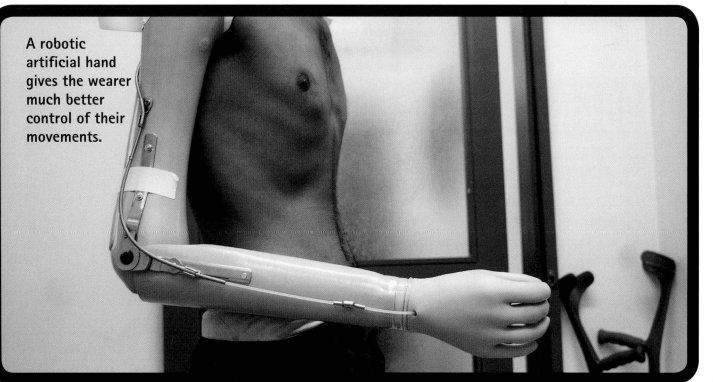

A robotic artificial hand gives the wearer much better control of their movements.

Robotic nurses

Could a robot nurse take care of patients in a hospital? Robots are not quite ready to replace human nurses. However, there are robots working in hospitals today.

Robot helper

Nurses are skilled at caring for patients. However, some of their daily work is dull and repetitive. It could be done by specially programmed robots. Helpmate is a robot designed to carry food, medicines, and X-rays. It runs on wheels, using a built-in map of the hospital. Its programming prevents it from bumping into people.

Care-O-bot is designed to help elderly patients.

Caring robots

Robots could also help people with a disability. Care-O-bot is a German robot designed to care for humans. It can obey commands to pick up and carry objects. It can even tidy up an area.

ROBOFACT

PENELOPE, THE ROBOT SCRUB NURSE

Scrub nurses handle **surgical instruments** and assist surgeons during operations. A one-armed robot called Penelope works successfully as a scrub nurse in the U.S.

Wakamaru is programmed with 10,000 words to help it communicate.

Caring for the elderly

No robot today can fully care for humans. However, robots like Wakamaru are the first step. Wakamaru is a Japanese robot that knows 10,000 words. It can talk to elderly people, helping keep them mentally alert.

Wakamaru has video cameras that can send images to caregivers or relatives. They can see that the owner is well. If the owner is quiet for too long, Wakamaru can say "Are you all right?" If necessary, it can call emergency services.

Yorisoi ifbot is another Japanese robot designed to look after elderly patients. Like Wakamaru, it knows many words. It is programmed to keep patients mentally active.

Future robotic nurses

A useful nursing robot would need the ability to move freely in a room containing people, beds, and equipment. It would need the ability to communicate with humans and understand spoken orders. Robots with these skills are coming, but are not ready yet.

Advances in robotic medicine

Robotic surgery is no longer new. Robots can do medical testing and simple nursing tasks. Will we ever see a robot doctor?

Advanced surgical robots

In 2006, for the first time, a surgical robot in Italy performed an operation without human help. This robot could one day be used in disaster zones, where many people need emergency surgery.

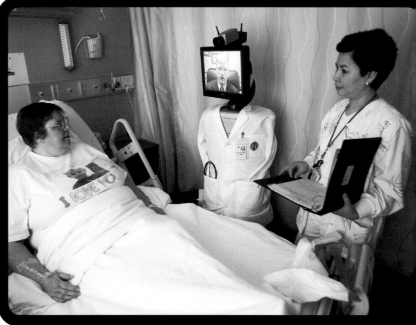

Medical robots can help doctors communicate with patients, even if the doctor is far away.

The future

In the distant future, there may be real robotic doctors. However, they would need a level of artificial intelligence that no robot has yet achieved.

The most likely medical advance is with artificial limbs. These will become more useful as they are fitted with robotic muscles and sensors.

ROBOFACT

ROBOTIC ARM

In 2005, Jesse Sullivan of Tennessee lost both arms in an accident. He was the first person fitted with a robotic arm controlled by his own nerves. He can now shave, feed himself, and throw a ball using the arm.

Up Close

ROBOT
Da Vinci surgical system

JOB
Surgical robot

MAKER
Intuitive Surgical, U.S.

SKILLS
Cutting and stitching,
three-dimensional video imaging

SIZE
59 inches (150 cm) long,
59 inches (150 cm) wide,
79 inches (200 cm) high

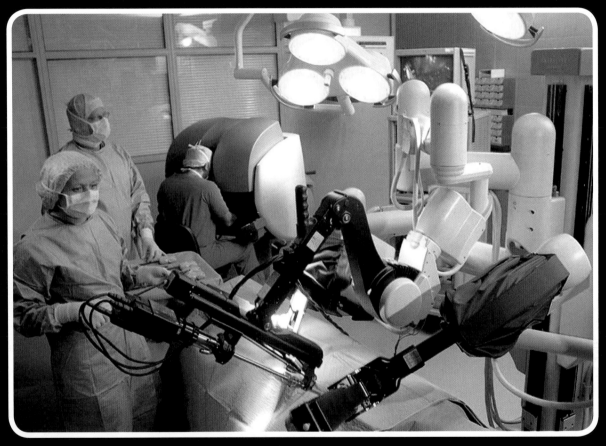

The da Vinci surgical system is a large four-armed robot. It makes very small incisions in the patient's body. Then, it inserts a tiny camera and robotic instruments to carry out operations.

A surgeon sits at a hooded workstation nearby, controlling the robot. The surgeon can see inside the patient through the robot's camera. The surgeon performs the operation using small joysticks and other controls. The robot can make very small movements that even a surgeon cannot. Even if the surgeon becomes tired during a long operation, the robot moves carefully and neatly.

Because the robot does less cutting than a surgeon would do in a normal operation, patients recover more quickly.

Robotics research

The study of robots is known as robotics. Robotics experts usually concentrate on one area, such as motion, sight, or touch.

Worldwide research

Thousands of researchers around the world study robotics. Many are teachers and students at universities. Others work for large companies that make robots, such as Honda and Unimate. At NASA, researchers develop robots for space exploration.

Spreading knowledge

No one can possibly know all there is to know about robots. Some researchers study robot movement. Other researchers are experts in artificial intelligence, robot vision, or grip control. Researchers learn from each other through meetings and conferences. They write books and magazine articles about their special area of robotics.

ROBOFACT

A NEW WORD FOR A NEW SCIENCE

The science fiction writer Isaac Asimov first used the word "robotics" in one of his books in the 1940s. At that time, there were no such things as robots, or robotics experts.

Robotics researchers build and test new robots.

Designing a robot

Even the simplest robots come from different people working together.
A robot needs several things to make it effective.

PURPOSE

Robots are always built for a purpose. Some are designed to perform a particular task, such as building a car or exploring Mars. Others are made to see if a new idea works, such as a robotic fish or snake.

INTELLIGENCE

Robots need to follow a set of instructions, stored on a computer chip. These instructions are prepared in a computer program. They give the robot artificial intelligence. The instructions can be changed and improved by altering the program.

SENSES

Some robots can see. Others rely on touch or pressure. If robots have no way to sense their environment, they cannot work effectively.

POWER

Robots rely on some form of power to operate their moving parts. Robots that move around on wheels or legs run on batteries. **Industrial** robots use **high voltage** electric power.

MOVING PARTS

All robots have some ability to move. Some roll on wheels or tracks. Others jump, swim, or fly. Many stay in one spot. They work with a single arm which can do a complicated task.

Artificial intelligence research

Some of the best-known robot research has been done at the Massachusetts Institute of Technology (MIT) Artificial Intelligence Laboratory. Researchers there are learning to make robots more intelligent.

Learning robots

Researchers at MIT try to create robots that can show emotions or learn from their environment. Two famous robots built at MIT are Kismet and Cog. Kismet has facial features that can show joy, sadness, and other emotions. Cog learned to pick things up, and examine them with its camera eyes.

Building better robots

Other researchers have learned from the work done at MIT. They are building robots that are even more advanced. This knowledge will be used in the future for intelligent robots.

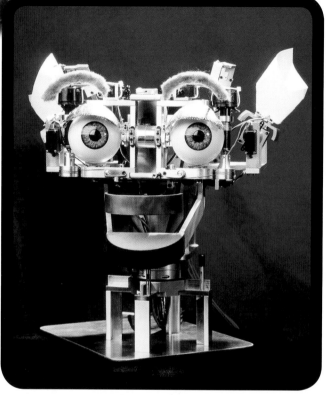

Kismet can show different facial expressions.

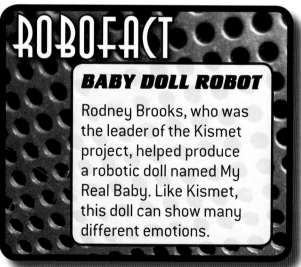

ROBOFACT

BABY DOLL ROBOT

Rodney Brooks, who was the leader of the Kismet project, helped produce a robotic doll named My Real Baby. Like Kismet, this doll can show many different emotions.

Up Close

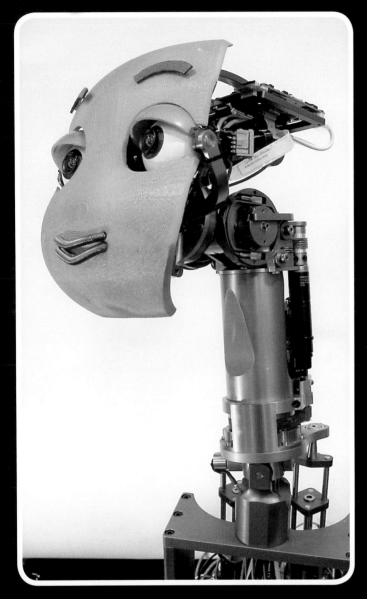

ROBOT
Mertz

JOB
Experimental robot head

MAKER
MIT Artificial Intelligence
Laboratory, U.S.

SKILLS
Interacting with humans,
curiosity, ability to learn

SIZE:
16 inches (40 cm) tall

Mertz is a robotic head. It is a more advanced version of robots such as Kismet and Cog. Its mouth, eyes, and eyebrows can all move, so it can show many different expressions.

Mertz is designed to learn by imitation, like a baby. It can learn to recognize human faces. It is friendly, but will learn to dislike people who annoy it.

Mertz will lean forward when it meets a new person and pull back when it is unhappy. Researchers put Mertz on display in public places. This helps it learn to recognize many different types of human faces.

The information researchers learn from Mertz will help them develop new robots. These robots will be able to recognize human beings and work with them.

Developing a humanoid robot

It takes many years to develop a robot from the first idea into a working machine. The Honda ASIMO can walk and run on two legs and obey simple instructions. It has taken many years to get to this level.

1986: First steps

Researchers at Honda started working on a two-legged robot in 1986. They first made Experimental Model 0 (E0). This was a pair of legs that could walk in a straight line. The researchers studied how humans walked. They used this knowledge to build better sets of legs, numbered E1 to E6.

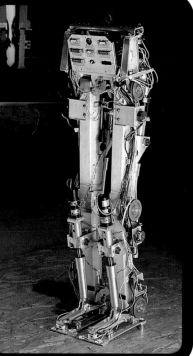

The original set of walking robotic legs from Honda.

1993: Adding a body

In 1993, Honda researchers built Prototype Model 1 (P1) and Prototype Model 2 (P2). These robots had heads, bodies, and arms. They could walk up and down stairs, or around in a circle. P2 had plastic skin to cover its gears and wiring. It was large and heavy, weighing 460 pounds (209 kg).

The P2 robot could walk, but it was slow and clumsy.

1997: Becoming independent

Once P2 was working, engineers built a smaller and lighter version, Prototype Model 3 (P3). This robot looked much more human. It was 63 inches (160 cm) tall and weighed 285 pounds (129 kg). It was the first completely independent **humanoid** robot.

The Honda P3 robot was completely independent.

2000: ASIMO

In 2000, Honda researchers built a much smaller and lighter robot. It is called ASIMO, which is short for **A**dvanced **S**tep in **I**nnovative **Mo**bility. The name also reminds us of Isaac Asimov, who wrote many of the first stories about robots. ASIMO is 47 inches (119 cm) tall and weighs 115 pounds (52 kg). It walks and runs like a human and can understand simple commands.

A modern ASIMO robot is small and compact.

The future for ASIMO

The ASIMO project has taken Honda many years and cost millions of dollars. The company hopes it will get the money back by producing thousands of ASIMO robots. These robots will be able to work in homes, offices, or factories.

Robot training

Robots of all types need to be trained to do their task. Training is a combination of computer programming and repeated practice.

Robot programming

Robots cannot do anything unless they have been programmed to do it. Robotics experts plan all the robot's movements in detail. Then they use a computer to write the robot's program. This program is loaded into the robot's onboard computer.

Movement and reactions

The program tells the robot the exact distances it must move and the exact angles at which its joints must bend. It tells the robot how to react to things it sees or touches.

A robot must be programmed before it can do anything.

ROBOFACT

TEACHING A ROBOT

One way of teaching a robot is to push it through each of its actions. Large industrial robots are often programmed this way. Workers hold the robot arm and guide it through a task. The robot records the movements in its computer and repeats them.

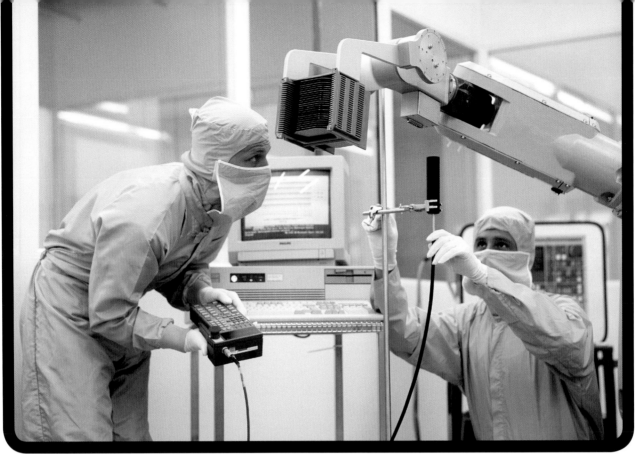

Programmers monitor their robot as it performs its tasks.

Adjusting the program

Once the main program has been written, the robotics experts see if it works. They start the robot and watch carefully. Sometimes the program works correctly and the robot does its task. But usually the programmers need to make changes. The robot may be reaching just a bit too far, or gripping an object too hard.

Thousands of commands

There are thousands of commands in a robot's program. The programmers and other robotics experts try each one. They make any changes that are necessary, and try again. Eventually, the robot does exactly what it is supposed to.

Virtual models

One way to speed up this process is to work with a **virtual model** of the robot. The virtual model can run through each part of the program. It moves just like the real robot would. If anything is not right, the programmer can see it immediately and fix the program.

Human or robot?

Some experts predict that by 2020 we will have robots that are as intelligent as humans. Others suggest that we could improve our bodies by adding robotic parts.

Artificial intelligence

Robotics experts are improving artificial intelligence in robots. Two types of artificial intelligence are expert systems and learning systems.

Modern toy robots, such as NeCoRo cats, have in-built learning systems.

Expert systems

Expert systems have all the knowledge needed to run one thing, such as an airline booking system. Expert systems control their specific area very well. However, they have no knowledge of anything except their special job.

Learning systems

Robots such as Sony's Aibo dog have learning systems. They can learn simple things, such as colors and shapes. Future robots could learn their way around a house, and learn to recognize their owners.

ROBOFACT

ROBOT SPEECH

Computer systems that recognize voices and understand words use a learning system. Future robots will need to learn so they can recognize their owner's voice.

Is this what robots will look like in the future?

Artificial limbs

Over the next few years, robotic limbs are likely to become stronger. Built-in computer chips will control wrist and finger joints. Artificial limbs will be controlled like natural limbs.

Artificial sight

Robotic vision is constantly improving. Some robots can detect colors and shapes. One day, we may have robotic eyes for blind people.

Other breakthroughs

In the future, other breakthroughs may be possible. People who rely on wheelchairs might one day be able to walk with robotic **implants** to control their legs.

The first artificial hearts were large and clumsy, and did not work well. Newer designs using robotic technology could be smaller and more effective.

Robotic humans?

In the distant future, humans may even develop robotic parts that are better than human bodies. The word "cyborg" comes from science fiction. It describes humans who have a mixture of natural and robotic body parts. Is that our future?

Become a robotics expert

There are many ways you can become a robotics expert. Here are just a few.

Learn more about robots

Look for books on robots in your library or bookstore. The World Wide Web has information on robots of every kind. Research laboratories and manufacturers all have Web sites with information about their latest work.

Make your own robot

Toy and hobby stores often sell small robot kits that you can build for yourself. Lego NXT kits are easy to assemble.

Learn to program your robot

Books and Web sites have information to help you program your robot. Programming is not easy at first, but you will soon understand the basics.

Make different kinds of robots

There are many sites on the World Wide Web for hobby robot builders. You can find instructions for tiny solar-powered robots called BEAM robots, and for CDbots made from old CDs.

Have fun!

Glossary

artificial limb - an artificial arm or leg

clean rooms - laboratories that are completely sealed to prevent contamination

contaminating - spoiling a substance by mixing other substances with it

disarm - to make an unexploded bomb safe

DNA - deoxyribonucleic acid; the part of the human body that carries genetic information such as hair color or eye color

high voltage - electricity that is much more powerful than household electricity

humanoid - similar in shape to a human

implants - devices that are surgically placed in the human body

incisions - cuts made by a surgeon or a surgical robot

industrial - used in a factory

laboratories - rooms where scientific tests and experiments are carried out

pressure sensors - electronic devices that detect and measure levels of pressure

program - to install the instructions that control a robot's actions

radioactive material - a substance that gives off dangerous rays of energy

science fiction - stories based on futuristic scientific ideas

silicon chips - tiny computer components made of a special material called silicon

surgery - the branch of medicine that treats disease or injury by performing operations

surgical instruments - scalpels, tweezers, and other instruments used by a surgeon

surgical robots - robots capable of performing surgical operations

test plates - flat, rectangular plates with wells that are used as small test tubes

virtual model - a three-dimensional model that appears on a computer screen

Index